CHURCH HISTORY WORKBOOK

C. Michael Patton &
Timothy G. Kimberley

Credo House

Credo House

PUBLISHERS

www.credohouse.org

Dedicated To:

Dr. John Hannah

Dr. Jeffrey Bingham

Dr. Justo Gonzalez

TABLE OF CONTENTS

F

Early Church   Medieval

70   529

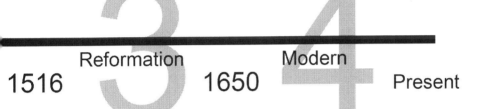

1516   Reformation   1650   Modern   Present

A Philosophy of Church History by C. Michael Patton

www.credohouse.org

TEENS

525-1517

ADOLESCENCE

325-524

INFANCY

100-325

DNA

-100

Early Church

Creedal Church

Medieval Church

All the building blocks of the church present with the completion of the Bible	A state of innocence and self-discovery as the church attempts to find and meet the expectations and requirements of being the Body of Christ	The church learns and begins to define itself in more definitive ways due to doctrinal reflection, internal controversy, and communal discovery	The church continues to grow, but moves in the direction of over-definition, authoritati● abuse, arrogance, bullyin● and rebellion

20s

1517-1900

30s & 40s

1900-Present

50s & BEYOND

Future

eformation Church

Mistakes of the past
re reflected upon and
begin to find remedy
through repentance,
formation,and renewed
purpose, hope,
and confidence

Postmodern Church

Reality and hope begins
to be adjusted due to
experience and unmet
expectations. Hope and
optimism become more
narrowed and focused or
abandoned completely

Future Church

Maturation in mind and thought
are brought into practice
as settlements are made
and values and convictions
become well-established though
knowledge and wisdom

1

Early Church

70   529

CHURCH HISTORY

EARLY CHURCH

70AD - 529AD

"If you suffer as a Christian, do not be ashamed, but praise God that you bear that name." (1 Pet. 4:16)

"The oftener we are mown down by you, the more in number we grow; the blood of Christians is seed."

- Tertullian (Apology, 50)

DEATH OF THE APOSTLES

1. James - Killed with a sword. 45 A.D.

2. Peter - Hung on a cross "head downward." A.D. 64

3. Andrew - Hung from an olive tree. A.D. 70

4. Thomas - Burned alive. A.D. 70

5. Phillip - Crucified. A.D. 54

6. Matthew - Beheaded. A.D. 65

7. Nathanael - Crucified. A.D. 70

8. James - Thrown from the temple. A.D. 63

9. Simon - Crucified. A.D. 74

10. Judas Thaddeus - Beaten with sticks. A.D. 72

11. Matthias - Stoned on a cross. A.D. 70

12. John - Natural death. A.D. 95

13. Paul - Beheaded. A.D. 69

Facts about martyrdom in the early church:

- Early believers were charged with atheism, cannibalism, and incest.

- Persecution often grew out of animosity by the populace rather than from deliberate government policy.

- Christians were blamed for causing natural disasters due to refusing to worship the deities that protected communities.

"A vast multitude [of Christians], were convicted, not so much of the crime of arson as of hatred of the human race. And in their deaths they were made the subjects of sport; for they were wrapped in the hides of wild beasts and torn to pieces by dogs, or nailed to crosses, or set on fire, and when day declined, were burned to serve for nocturnal lights."

-Tacitus' Annals XV.44

PERSECUTIONS

Peter
Paul

Clement of Rome
John (exiled)

Ignatius
Polycarp   Justin Martyr

Perpetua and Felicity
Irenaeus   Hippolytus

Origen   Cyprian   Mauritius

Nero	Domitian	Trajan	Marcus Aurelius	Septimus Severus	Maximinus the Thracian	Decius	Valerian	Diocletian
64	90-96	98-117	161-180	201-211	235-236	249-251	257-260	303-311

LABELLUS: A CERTIFICATE DEMONSTRATING THAT ONE HAD MADE THE APPROPRIATE SACRIFICES TO THE GODS OF ROME.

Sacrificati: Describes those who had actually offered a sacrifice to the idols. If a Christian made sacrifices and obtained a labellus, they were only offered absolution on their deathbeds.

Libellatici: Describes those who had false labellus created without actually making the sacrafices. A two year sanction was imposed as penance.

Traditores: Describes those who gave up scriptures and/or revealed names of fellow Christians. From Latin tradere - *"hand over; deliver; betray"*

Polycarp was brought before the proconsul, who begged him to have respect for his great age (he was probably nearly 100), saying, "Swear by the genius of Caesar" and denounce "the atheists." But Polycarp, seeing "the lawless heathen" in the amphitheater, "waved his hands at them, and looked up to heaven with a groan and said, 'Away with the atheists.' " The proconsul persisted, "Swear, and I will release you. Curse Christ." And Polycarp replied, **"Eighty-six years have I served him, and he has done me no wrong; how can I blaspheme my King who saved me?"** He was condemned to death and burned alive.

Popular opinion about Christianity began to change in the late third century as people witnessed the steadfast commitment of Christians to die for their faith.

Name	Dates	Place	Works	Facts
Clement of Rome	c.30 – c. 100	Rome	1 Clement	Possibly knew Paul and Peter
Ignatius	d. 117	Antioch	Ephesians Magnesians Trallians	Letters written in route to martyrdom Opposed Gnosticism
Shepherd of Hermas	Late 1st century	Rome	The Shepherd	Wrote in visions and parables
Barnabas	Late 1st century	Alexandria	Epistle of Barnabas	Wrote in allegory
Papias	c. 60 – c. 130	Hierapolis	Exposition of the Oracles of Our Lord	Knew John Was premillenial Claimed Mark's Gospel
Polycarp	c. 69 – 160	Smyrna	Philippians	Knew John

APOSTOLIC FATHERS

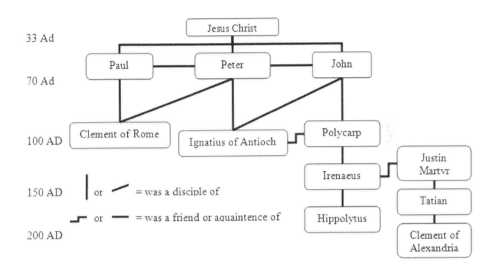

Facts about faith in the early church:

- Most of the leaders were pastoral.

- Most elements of faith were in "seed form".

- Much time was spent trying to give a defense of Christian behavior to political leaders.

- Practical leadership was the primary concern.

- Establishment of the "Rule of Faith"

- Catechumen (new converts) were expected to go through three years of training before being baptized.

EDICT OF MILAN

Edict agreed upon by
Emperors Constantine and
Licinius which legalized
Christianity, granting them
restitution of lands and
property.

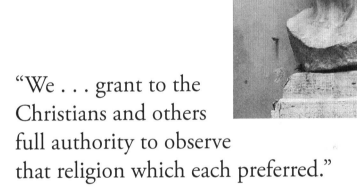

"We . . . grant to the
Christians and others
full authority to observe
that religion which each preferred."

-Constantine and Licinius

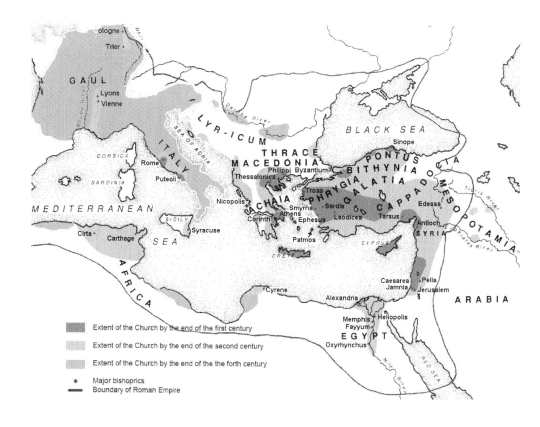

Extent of the Church by the end of the first century

Extent of the Church by the end of the second century

Extent of the Church by the end of the the forth century

• Major bishoprics
— Boundary of Roman Empire

Arius:

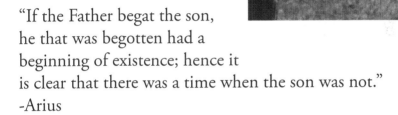

Believed that Christ is not eternally God but a creation of God the Father, having his genesis/"begotteness" in eternity past. He is the first created being.

"If the Father begat the son, he that was begotten had a beginning of existence; hence it is clear that there was a time when the son was not."
-Arius

The uncreated God has made the Son
A beginning of things created,
And by adoption has God made the Son
Into an advancement of himself.
Yet the Son's substance is
Removed from the substance of the Father:
The Son is not equal to the Father,
Nor does he share the same substance.
God is the all-wise Father,
And the Son is the teacher of his mysteries.
The members of the Holy Trinity
Share unequal glories.

Athanasius:
298 – 373

Bishop of Alexandria for 45 years, 17 of which were spent in five exiles due to the instigation of four emperors. He is best known for his stance against Arianism as an ardent defender of the Trinity.

Council of Nicea
325AD

The first "Ecumenical Council", called by Emperor Constantine to solve the religious division of the empire brought about by the Arian controversy.

Does it make one iota of difference?

Nicea	o`moousioj homoousios
Arius	o`moiousioj homoiousios

Nicene Creed

We believe in one God, the Father, the Almighty [pantokratora], creator of all that is seen and unseen. We believe in one Lord, Jesus Christ, the only Son of God, eternally begotten [pro panton ton aionon] of the Father, God from God, Light from Light, true God from true God, begotten, not made, of the same essence [homoousion] with the Father.

Fables about Nicea

- It is illegitimate because it was called by a civil authority.

- The doctrine of the Trinity was invented then.

- Constantine forced the bishops to agree.

- It was a close vote.

DISCUSSION QUESTIONS:

1. WE ARE NOW 25% INTO CHURCH HISTORY. WHAT ARE SOME THINGS THAT SURPRISED YOU ABOUT THIS FIRST SESSION?

2. DO YOU THINK YOU WOULD HAVE ENDURED THE PERSECUTIONS OF THE EARLY CHURCH? HOW WOULD YOU HAVE DEALT WITH PEOPLE WHO DENIED CHRIST DURING PERSECUTION BUT RE-TURNED TO THE CHURCH ONCE IT WAS SAFE?

3. IS THE ISSUE OF THE TRINITY AS IMPORTANT AS THE EARLY CHURCH THOUGHT?

4. WHAT IS THE BIGGEST THING YOU WILL TAKE AWAY FROM LEARNING ABOUT THE EARLY CHURCH?

2

Medieval

529   1516

CHURCH HISTORY

MEDIEVAL CHURCH

529AD - 1516AD

Council of Nicea (325; 381)

Council of Chalcedon (451)

Council of Orange (529)

regula fide
"rule of faith"

Refers to the concept that there is a historic tradition regulating orthodox belief to which all Christians have always subscribed. This rule of faith is expressed through creeds and confessions.

Vincentian Canon

"That which has been believed always, everywhere, and by all."

Apostolic Succession

The unbroken succession which sustains the orthodox faith through the centuries. Those who fall within this line can trace their teachings back to the Apostles.

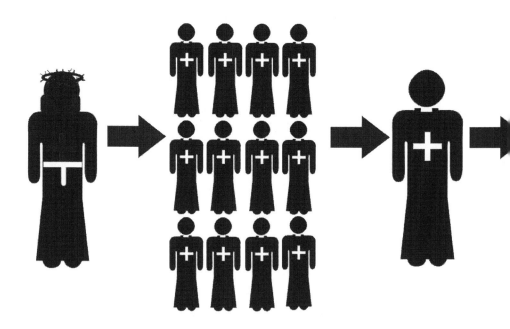

Catholic Understanding:
- Succession in person (i.e. Popes and Bishops)

Protestant Understanding:
- Succession in teaching

Rise of the Papacy:

Leo I meets Attila the Hun in 450 A.D.

Rise of the Papacy:

Leo III crowns Charlemagne on December 25, 800 A.D.

Rise of the Papacy

Corruption of the *regula fide.*

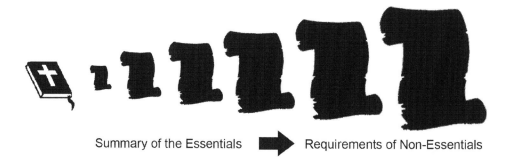

Summary of the Essentials ➡ Requirements of Non-Essentials

Event	Year
Latin used in prayer and worship imposed by Gregory I	600
Prayers directed to Mary, dead saints, and angels	600
Kissing the pope's feet began with Pope Constantine	709
Veneration of cross, images, and relics authorized	786
College of Cardinals established	927
Canonization of dead people as saints	995
Attendance at Mass made mandatory	1000
Celibacy of priesthood decreed by Pope Gregory VII	1079
The sale of indulgences established to reduce time in Purgatory	1090
Transubstantiation proclaimed by Pope Innocent	1215
Doctrine of the seven sacraments affirmed	1215
Infallibility of the papacy firmly pushed by Pope John XXII	1324
Tradition claimed equal in authority to the Bible at the Council of Trent	1545
Apocryphal book declared canon by Council of Trent	1546

SEVEN SACRAMENTS

1. Baptism
- New birth that removes original sin, placing people in a right relationship with God

2. Confirmation
- A believer receives the Holy Spirit by the laying on of hands

3. Eucharist
- Sacrifice of Christ in which the believer receives forgiveness of venial sins

4. Penance
- Confession of sins to a priest in order to receive forgiveness and punishment (exclusion from Mass, alms giving, fasting, etc.)

5. Extreme Unction
- An administration of grace given to a dying person through anointing with oil in order to prepare the person's soul for heaven

6. Holy Orders
- Ordination of a priest giving them the power to administer the sacraments

7. Matrimony
- The exchange of vows of union between a man and a woman performed by a priest

extra ecclesiam nulla salus
"outside the Church there is no salvation"

"We are compelled in virtue of our faith to believe and maintain that there is only one holy Catholic Church, and that one is apostolic. This we firmly believe and profess without qualification. Outside this Church there is no salvation and no remission of sins. . . .

Furthermore, we declare, we proclaim, we define that it is absolutely necessary for salvation that every human creature be subject to the Roman Pontiff."

-Pope Boniface VIII, Bull Unam sanctam (1302)

Five Bishoprics of the Early Church

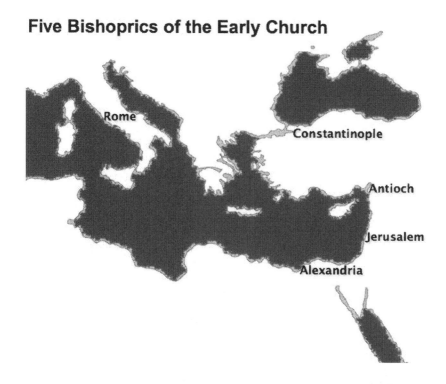

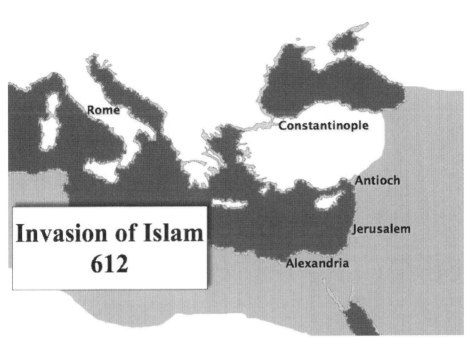

Rome

Constantinople

Antioch

Jerusalem

Alexandria

**Invasion of Islam
612**

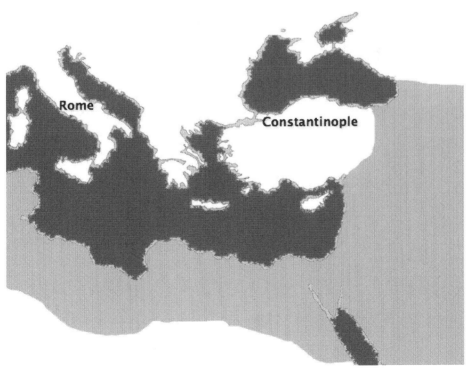

Rome

Constantinople

THE GREAT SCHISM 1054AD

Reasons for the schism

- Rome's claim to supremacy
- Distinction and suppression of language
- Distinction in philosophy
- Filioque
- Atrocities of the Fourth Crusade

filioque "and the son"

Western Church addition to the Nicene Creed at Third Council of Toledo (589; officially 1014) which expressed that the Holy Spirit proceeded from the Father and the Son.

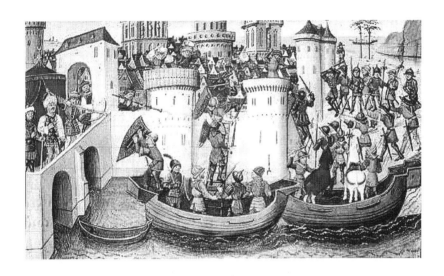

Fourth Crusade (1202-1204)

Eastern Church called on their brothers in the West to come to their aid as the Muslim invasion was bringing immanent destruction.

Instead of coming to their rescue, "crusaders" sacked Constantinople, pillaged their land, and raped the women.

```
                                              Western Church
One, Holy, Catholic, Apostolic Church  <
                                              Eastern Orthodox
```

Characteristics of Eastern Orthodoxy

- Doctrine does not seek progression but ancient identification

- Often referred to as the church of the seven councils

- Seeks mystery above reason

- Liturgy is the Gospel lived

- Rejects Purgatory

- Seeks divination

DISCUSSION QUESTIONS:

1. WHAT ASPECTS OF THE SECOND SESSION REALLY STAND OUT TO YOU?

2. WHAT ARE SOME WAYS A KNOWLEDGE OF THE MEDIEVAL PERIOD CAN BE BENEFICIAL FOR YOUR WALK WITH GOD TODAY? WHAT IS AT STAKE, POSITIVELY AND NEGATIVELY, IF WE IGNORE THE MEDIEVAL PERIOD?

3. WHAT DO YOU THINK ABOUT THE DIFFERENCE BETWEEN A ROMAN CATHOLIC AND PROTESTANT VIEW OF APOSTOLIC SUCCESSION?

4. DO YOU THINK IT WAS JUSTIFIABLE FOR THE GREAT SCHISM TO TAKE PLACE? DO YOU THINK CHRISTIANS SHOULD TRY TO LOOK PAST DIFFERENCES AND TRY TO COME BACK TOGETHER INTO ONE UNIFIED CHURCH?

Reformation
1516   1650

CHURCH HISTORY

REFORMATION CHURCH

1516AD - 1650AD

Preparation for Reformation

1. Internal Preparation

2. External Preparation

1. INTERNAL PREPARATION

Pre-Reformers

1. John Wycliffe
(ca. 1329-1384)

Oxford professor who challenged the authority of the Pope, translated the Bible into English.

Contentions:
- Jesus, not the Pope was the head of the Church.

- The Ecclesiatical authority was saturated with greed and immorality and needed reform.

- Placed the authority of the Bible above that of the Church.

1. INTERNAL PREPARATION

Pre-Reformers

2. John Huss
(ca. 1373-1415)

Professor of philosophy at the University of Prague who sought to reform the doctrine and practices of the Catholic church.

Contentions:

- Christ, not the Pope, is the head of the church.

- Simony is immoral.

- Condemned and burned at the stake.

Fall of the Papacy

During the 12th and 13th centuries, the power of the Pope reached its zenith, with the King of France, England, and Emperor merely serving as the Pope's marshals. He held the keys to the kingdom of heaven in heaven and on earth. Rome was seen as the fountain head for the conversion of all of Europe.

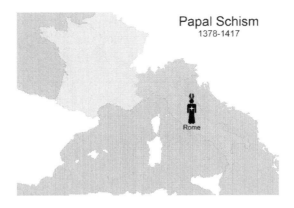

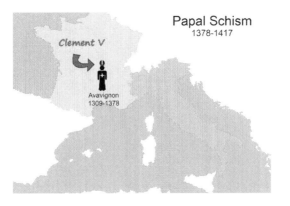

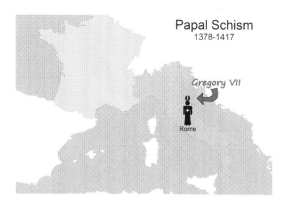

Papal Schism
1378-1417

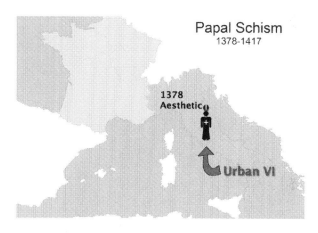

Papal Schism
1378-1417

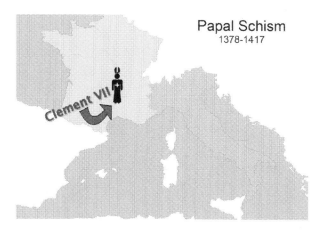

Papal Schism
1378-1417

1. INTERNAL PREPARATION

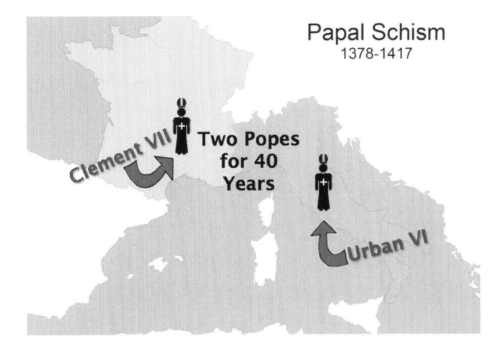

Fall of the Papacy

The Western Schism (1378-1415):
Civil leaders bartered for the sale of their allegiance.

With so much uncertainty, loyalty to one's nation began to displace loyalty to the church as primary.

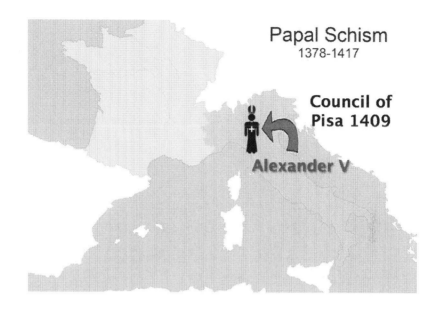

Papal Schism
1378-1417

Council of
Pisa 1409

Alexander V

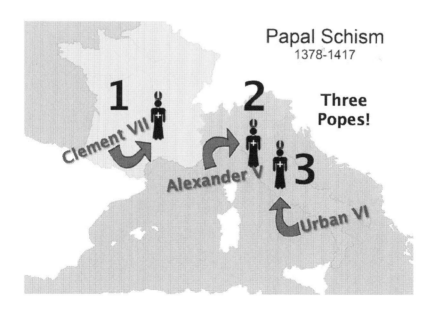

Papal Schism
1378-1417

Three
Popes!

1

2

3

Clement VII

Alexander V

Urban VI

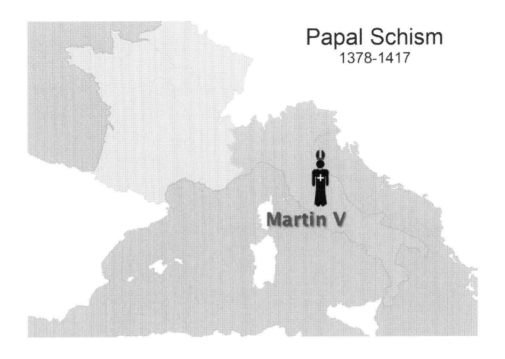

Papal Schism
1378-1417

Martin V

"God has given us the Papacy, let us enjoy it."

-Pope Leo X

Renaissance Papacy:

- One Pope back in Rome.

- Papal moral reform did not happen.

- Alexander VI (1492-1503), part of the Borgia family, openly flaunted his immorality and promoted his children to offices in the church. He appointed his nine-year-old son as a cardinal.

2. EXTERNAL PREPARATION

Hundred Year War Between England and France:

The Papacy being moved to France during the Avignon Papacy would serve to make English reform more palatable.

Black Death (Bubonic Plague):

Between 1347-1351 killed between one-third and one half of Europe's population.

Outbreaks for the next 120 years.

By 1450 Europe's population was down seventy-percent.

Danse Macabre: "dance of death"

Der Apt.

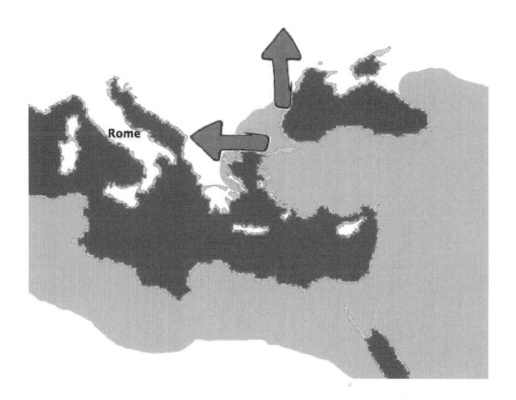

Invasion of Islam into Constantinople:

Byzantine Christians fled West bringing a store-house of ancient writing, manuscripts, and Biblical text.

Invention of the Printing Press (1439):

Facilitated the ideas of the Enlightenment.

Facilitated the distribution of Scripture.

Facilitated a revival of learning.

THE GREAT REFORMATION

Martin Luther (1483-1546)

German Augustinian monk who is known as the father of the Reformation.

Luther's Early Life:

- Neurotic obsession with his own guilt.

- Commissioned to teach study the New Testament and teach theology by Johann von Staupitz.

- Discovery: while studying the book of Romans, he came upon Romans 1:17.

For in the gospel the righteousness of God is revealed - a righteousness that is by faith from first to last, just as it is written: "The righteous will live by faith." - Romans 1:17

Indulgences:

In 1516–17, Johann Tetzel, a Dominican friar and papal commissioner for indulgences, was sent to Germany by the Roman Catholic Church to sell indulgences to raise money to rebuild St. Peter's Basilica.

"When the coin in the coffer rings, a soul from Purgatory springs"

"Sobald der Gülden im Becken klingt im huy die Seel im Himmel springt "

St. Peters Basillica

Nailing of 95 Thesis (1517):

- Ninety-five complaints about the Church and the papacy.

- Meant to bring about internal debate. Doctrinal and moral.

Nailing of 95 Thesis (1517):

6. The pope himself cannot remit guilt, but only declare and confirm that it has been remitted by God.

27. There is no divine authority for preaching that the soul flies out of purgatory immediately when the money clinks in the bottom of the chest.

82. Why does not the pope liberate everyone from purgatory for the sake of love (a most holy thing) and because of the supreme necessity of their souls? This would be morally the best of all reasons. Meanwhile he redeems innumerable souls for money, a most perishable thing, with which to build St. Peter's church, a very minor purpose.

"Unless I am convinced by proofs from Scriptures or by plain and clear reasons and arguments, I can and will not retract, for it is neither safe nor wise to do anything against conscience. Here I stand. I can do no other. God help me. Amen."

- Diet of Worms (1521)

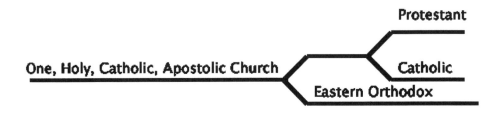

Five Solas of the Reformation

Sola Scriptura

Sola Fide

Sola Gratia

Solus Christus

Soli Deo gloria

Luke 23:44-46

It was now about the sixth hour, and darkness fell over the whole land until the ninth hour, because the sun was obscured; and the veil of the temple was torn in two. And Jesus, crying out with a loud voice, said, "Father, INTO YOUR HANDS I COMMIT MY SPIRIT." Having said this, He breathed His last.

MEDIEVAL CHURCH

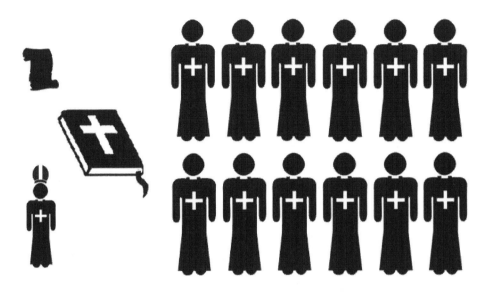

GREAT REFORMATION

1 Peter 2:9

But you are a chosen people, a royal priesthood, a holy nation, a people belonging to God, that you may declare the praises of him who called you out of darkness into his wonderful light.

DISCUSSION QUESTIONS

1. IF WYCLIFFE AND HUSS LIVED TODAY WHAT DO YOU THINK THEY WOULD TRY TO REFORM ABOUT THE CHURCH OF OUR DAY?

2. LOOKING AT ALL THE EXTERNAL PREPARATION LEADING TO THE REFORMATION, WHAT THINGS ARE HAPPENING IN OUR WORLD OUTSIDE OF THE CHURCH THAT MIGHT LEAD TO A NEW REFORMATION?

3. OF THE FIVE SOLAS OF THE REFORMATION, WHICH ONE WOULD YOU WANT TO BE GREATER IN YOUR LIFE?

4. WHAT IS THE BIGGEST THING YOU WILL TAKE AWAY FROM LEARNING ABOUT THE REFORMATION?

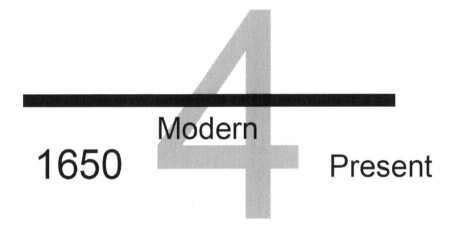

CHURCH HISTORY

MODERN CHURCH

1650AD - PRESENT

1. Modernism

2. Liberalism

3. Fundamentalism

4. Evangelicalism

5. Postmodernism

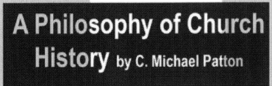

A Philosophy of Church History by C. Michael Patton

www.credohouse.org

TEENS

ADOLESCENCE

325-524

INFANCY

100-325

DNA

-100

DNA

All the building blocks of the church present with the completion of the Bible

Early Church

A state of innocence and self-discovery as the church attempts to find and meet the expectations and requirements of being the Body of Christ

Creedal Church

The church learns and begins to define itself in more definitive ways due to doctrinal reflection, internal controversy, and communal discovery

Medieval Church

The church continues to grow, but moves in the direction of over-definition, authorita abuse, arrogance, bully and rebellion

20s

1517-1900

30s & 40s

1900-Present

50s & BEYOND

Future

eformation Church

Mistakes of the past
re reflected upon and
begin to find remedy
through repentance,
ormation,and renewed
purpose, hope,
and confidence

Postmodern Church

Reality and hope begins
to be adjusted due to
experience and unmet
expectations. Hope and
optimism become more
narrowed and focused or
abandoned completely

Future Church

Maturation in mind and thought
are brought into practice
as settlements are made
and values and convictions
become well-established though
knowledge and wisdom

MODERNISM

Rene Descartes (1596-1650)

"Father of Modern Philosophy" who introduced the "Cartesian method" of inquiry which required indubitability (absolute certainty) in all areas of life.

cogito ergo sum
"I think therefore I am"

The new Philosophy calls all in doubt,
The Element of fire is quite put out;
The Sun is lost, and th'earth, and no man's wit
Can well direct him where to look for it
-John Donne

Doubt Everything!

Scientific Revolution

1. Earth is not the center of universe; Sun is the center of the solar system

2. Scientific method

3. Discoveries in anatomy

4. Language of mathematics and geometry

5. Laws of nature discovered

6. The authority of science and reason began to replace the authority of the church and Scripture

Higher Criticism:

A branch of biblical studies that flourished in Germany in the 18th and 19th centuries which sought to apply the principles of the Enlightenment, scientific inquiry, and modern philosophy to the text of the Scriptures.

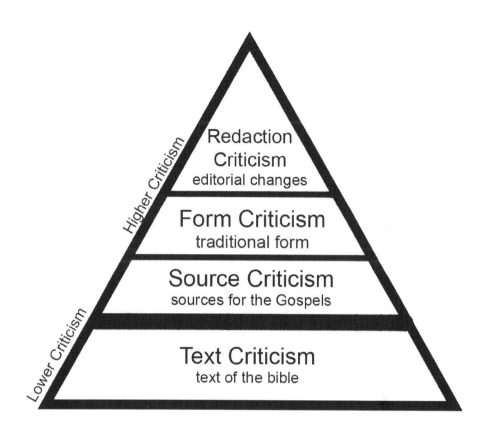

Demythologization:

The process most famously used by Thomas Jefferson to remove from the Bible all the elements that seemed mythological.

Quest for the Historic Jesus:

Movement in Biblical studies which sought to separate the Jesus from faith from the Jesus of history (Albert Schweitzer).

Charles Darwin
(1809-1882)

Father of Darwinian Evolution which gave people an alternative and scientific explanation for the origin of species.

Four pivotal issues for Darwin:

- Flightless birds (rhea)

- Goose with webbed feet that never went into the water

- Ichneumonidae wasp who laid its eggs in a caterpillar in a painful process

- Death of his 11-year-old daughter

"Evolution made it possible to be
an intellectually satisfied atheist."
-Richard Dawkins

Liberalism: A movement birthed out of modern-ism which sought to "save" Christianity (and reli-gion in general) from the damage caused by mod-ernistic thinking by adapting it essence.

Friedrich Schleiermacher
(1768-1834)

Father of Theological
Liberalism who expressed
his faith not as rational
belief, but as a feeling of
dependence on God.

"You reject the dogmas and propositions of religion.... Religion does not need them; it is only human reflection on the content of our religious feelings or affections.... Do you say that you cannot accept miracles, revelation, inspiration? You are right; we are children no longer; the time for fairy-tales is past."

-Friedrich Schleiermacher

Ecumenicalism:

Sought to bring unity to the church under the banner of moral cause rather than doctrinal creed. This movement is represented most by the World Council of Churches.

	Liberalism	Historic Christianity
Essence of Christianity	Morality	Christ redemption
Scripture	Mythology	God's word
Christ	Example to be followed	God to be worshipped
God	Love	Love and Justice
Ultimate authority	Experience and reason	Bible
Man	Essentially good	Morally fallen
Sin	Vestiges of perverse animal instincts	Rebellion against God
Salvation	Good works	Faith in Christ
Church	Concerned with world and society (Social Gospel)	Concerned with the salvation of souls.
Eschatology	No hell, all "saved"	God's judgment, Christians saved

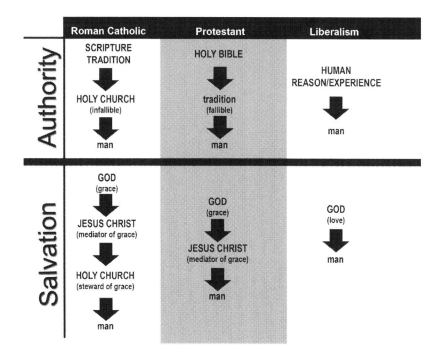

"A God without wrath brought men without sin into a kingdom without judgment through the ministrations of a Christ without a cross."

-H. Richard Niebuhr

"A chorus of ecumenical voices keep harping the unity tune. What they are saying is, "Christians of all doctrinal shades and beliefs must come together in one visible organization, regardless... Unite, unite!" Such teaching is false, reckless and dangerous. Truth alone must determine our alignments. Truth comes before unity."

-Charles H. Spurgeon

Fundamentalism: A movement in the early 21st century which sought to rescue Christianity from liberalism, restoring and defending the fundamental creeds of the Christian faith.

The Fundamentals, published from 1915-1920, was a monumental work of 90 essays contained in twelve volumes. Drawing from dozens of authors including James Orr, B.B. Warfield, and G. Campbell Morgan, these essays defended the essence---the Fundamentals---of the Christian faith against the threat of Liberalism.

OLD SCHOOLS

Princeton
(1746; Presbyterian)

Harvard
(1636; Calvinist)

Yale (1701; Calvinist)

Dartmouth
(1769;
Congregationalist)

Brown (1746; Baptist)

NEW SCHOOLS

Wheaton College
(1860)

Westminster Theological Seminary
(1929)

Dallas Theological
Seminary (1924)

Fuller Theological
Seminary (1947)

Scopes Monkey Trial (1925):

A nationally publicized trial which shaped and defined Fundamentalism as an anti-intellectual "back-woods" religion that resisted scientific reality in favor of cultish beliefs.

Williams Jennings Bryan disappeared from public life and died in his sleep five days after winning the verdict.

Fundamentalism disappeared from culture and died in the court of influence.

Fundamentalism:

- No tolerance for any compromise.

- Became defined more by non-essential morals than doctrines.

- Don't drink, don't smoke, don't dance, and don't play cards, don't go to movies.

- Left the Universities and started their own schools.

- Became separatists and "cultish Christianity"; "A holy nation". No longer a "kingdom of priests".

Evangelicalism (American): A movement in conservative Christianity which responded to the treats of Liberalism and Fundamentalism by seeking to engage culture with the Gospel without compromising the essentials.

Fundamentalism: "Orthodoxy gone cultic."
-Edward J. Carnell

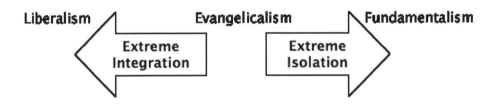

third way (tertium quid)

Liberalism   Evangelicalism   Fundamentalism

Extreme
Integration

Extreme
Isolation

"Our New York Campaign has been challenged by some extremists on two points. First as to sponsorship, I would like to make myself clear. I intend to go anywhere, sponsored by anybody, to preach the Gospel of Christ, if there are no strings attached to my message. I am sponsored by civic clubs, universities, ministerial associations and councils of churches all over the world. I intend to continue" (Christian Beacon, April 4, 1957).

POSTMODERNISM

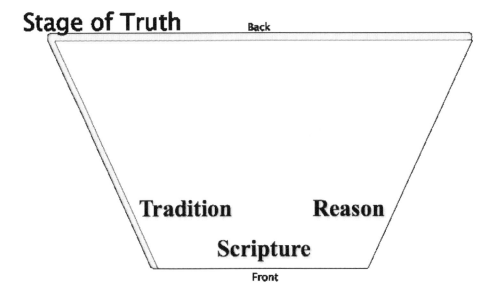

DISCUSSION QUESTIONS

1. WHAT DO YOU THINK ABOUT DARWIN'S FOUR PIVOTAL ISSUES? IF DARWIN SAT DOWN WITH YOU AT A COFFEE SHOP WHAT WOULD YOU SAY TO HIM?

2. WHAT ARE SOME WAYS YOU SEE SCHLEIERMACH-ER'S INFLUENCE IN OUR WORLD?

3. WHAT IS THE BIGGEST THING YOU WILL TAKE AWAY FROM LEARNING ABOUT THE MODERN CHURCH?

4. LET'S LOOK BACK OVER OUR ENTIRE 2,000 YEAR STUDY. WHAT ARE SOME OF THE HIGH-LIGHTS?

CREDOHOUSE.ORG

twitter.com/credohouse

facebook.com/credohouse

Credo House

PUBLISHERS

www.credohouse.org

14659553R00049

Made in the USA
Charleston, SC
24 September 2012